6 STUDIES FOR INDIVIDUALS OR GROUPS

Receiving Peace *from God*

PEACE

[DALE &
JUANITA RYAN]

Letting God Be God Bible Studies

InterVarsity Press
Downers Grove, Illinois

InterVarsity Press
P.O. Box 1400, Downers Grove, IL 60515-1426
World Wide Web: www.ivpress.com
E-mail: mail@ivpress.com

*InterVarsity Press® is the book-publishing division of InterVarsity Christian Fellowship/USA®, a student
movement active on campus at hundreds of universities, colleges and schools of nursing in the United
States of America, and a member movement of the International Fellowship of Evangelical Students.
For information about local and regional activities, write Public Relations Dept., InterVarsity
Christian Fellowship/USA, 6400 Schroeder Rd., P.O. Box 7895, Madison, WI 53707-7895.*

Cover photograph: Michael Goss

Cover logo and interior icons: Roberta Polfus

ISBN 0-8308-2077-9

Printed in the United States of America ∞

19	18	17	16	15	14	13	12	11	10	9	8	7	6	5	4	3	2	1
16	15	14	13	12	11	10	09	08	07	06	05	04	03	02	01			

Contents

INTRODUCTION: RECEIVING PEACE FROM GOD

And he will be called
  Wonderful Counselor, Mighty God,
  Everlasting Father, Prince of Peace.
(Isaiah 9:6)

Why is life so stressful? Why are we so tense, so tired? We may not be completely aware that our tension and exhaustion are signs that we live with deep fears and anxieties. They are signals that our hearts and minds are not at peace. Or perhaps we are aware of this, but we don't know how to get past our fears. We don't know how to experience genuine inner peace.

Many things can mimic peace that are not really peace at all. Avoidance, denial and pretense can all look like peace. But peace is more than an absence of conflict. Peace between people grows out of fairness and equity. It is the byproduct of living respectfully with each other. Another way of saying this is that peace grows in the soil of love—love which seeks fairness and mercy, love that is compassionate and genuinely valuing of others.

Our internal peace is also something that grows in the soil of love. Internal peace comes from knowing that we are held in the compassionate, merciful heart of God. The Scriptures tell us that the God of peace is with us. "Letting God be God" means letting God be the source of our peace. It means knowing ourselves to be held in God's strong, tender love.

Sometimes, of course, we fear that we are not loved by God. The journey toward a life of peace is a journey that takes us through those fears and back to the truth of who God is.

The studies in this guide are designed to help you receive God's peace and live life with God's gift of peace deep within you. God's gift of peace is more than a stress-reduction program. God's gift of peace is far more substantial than a warm feeling. Essentially, God's gift of peace is the product of sinking your roots deeply into the soil of God's love.

It is our prayer that in the process of working through these studies, you will be able to receive God's peace in new ways.

Learning to Let God Be God

The Bible studies in this series are based on three basic convictions. The first of these convictions is that we are by our very nature dependent on our Maker. We need God. We need God's help with the daily challenges of life. We need God's love, peace, forgiveness, guidance and hope. The invitation to "let God be God" is an invitation to let God be who God really is. But it is also an invitation to us to be who we really are—God's deeply loved children.

Second, these studies are based on the conviction that God is willing, ready and eager to be God in our lives. God is not distant, inaccessible or indifferent. Rather, God is actively involved, offering us all that we need. God offers us all the love, strength, hope and peace we need.

Finally, these studies are based on the conviction that the spiritual life begins with receiving from God. What we do when we "let God be God" is receive from God the good gifts that God is eager to give to us. God has offered to love us. We are "letting God be God" when we receive this love. God has offered to guide us. We are "letting God be God" when we receive this guidance. Receiving from God is the starting point of the spiritual life. There is, of course, a place in the Christian journey for giving to God—a place for commitment and dedication. But if we have not learned well to receive from God, then we will almost certainly experience the Christian journey to be full of heavy burdens.

These are basic Christian convictions that closely resemble the first three steps of the twelve steps of Alcoholics Anonymous. The short summary is "I can't. God can. I'll let him." These are spiritual truths that apply to all of our lives. They may seem pretty simple. But most of us find that actually doing them—putting these truths into practice—is anything but simple. The problem is that receiving is not instinctive for most of us. What is instinctive is self-sufficiency, independence and managing by ourselves. What comes naturally is trying harder and trying our hardest. Letting go of this performance-oriented spirituality and allowing ourselves to receive from God will be a challenging adventure for most of us. It is the adventure that is at the heart of these Bible studies.

These Bible studies are designed to help you explore what it means to receive from God—what it means to let God be God in your life. George MacDonald used a wonderful metaphor when talking about the process of learning to receive from God. He said, "There are good things God must delay giving, until his child has a pocket to hold them—until God gets his child to make that pocket" (as cited in Michael R. Phillips, ed., *Discovering the Character of God* [Minneapolis: Bethany House, 1989], p. 156). These studies are designed to help you sew some new pockets that are big enough to hold the abundant good gifts that God has prepared for you.

Getting the Most from These Studies

The guides in this series are designed to assist you to find out what the Bible has to say about God and to grow in your ability to "let God be God" in your life. The passages you study will be thought provoking, challenging, inspiring and very personal. It will become obvious that these studies are not designed merely to convince you of the truthfulness of some idea. And they won't provide a systematic presentation of everything the Bible says about any subject. Rather, they will create an opportunity for biblical truths to renew your heart and mind.

There are six studies in each guide. Our hope is that this will provide you with maximum flexibility in how you use these guides. Combining the guides in various ways will allow you to adapt them to your time schedule and to focus on the concerns most important to you or your group.

All of the studies in this series use a workbook format. Space is provided for writing responses to each question. This is ideal for personal study and allows group members to prepare in advance for the discussion. The guides also contain notes with suggestions on how to lead a group discussion. The notes provide additional background information on certain questions, give helpful tips on group dynamics and suggest ways to deal with problems that may arise during the discussion. These features equip someone with little or no experience to lead an effective discussion.

Suggestions for Individual Study

1. As you begin each study, pray that God would give you wisdom and courage through his Word.

2. After spending time in preparation, read and reread the passage to be studied.

3. Write your responses in the space provided or in a personal journal. Writing can bring clarity and deeper understanding of yourself and God's Word. For the same reason, we suggest that you write out your prayers at various points in each study.

4. Most of the studies include questions that invite you to spend time in meditative prayer. The biblical text is communication addressed personally to us. Meditative prayer can enrich and deepen your experience of a biblical text.

5. After you have completed your study of the passage, you might want to read the leader's notes at the back of the guide to gain additional insight and information.

6. Share what you are learning with someone you trust. If you are not able to use these guides in a group you might want to consider participating in one of our online discussion groups at <www.lettinggodbegod.com>.

Suggestions for Group Study

Even if you have already done these studies individually, we strongly encourage you to find some way to do them with a group of other people as well. Although each person's journey is different, everyone's journey is empowered by the mutual support and encouragement that can only be found in a one-on-one or group setting. Several reminders may be helpful for participants in a group study.

1. Trust grows over time. If opening up in a group setting feels risky, realize that you do not have to share more than what feels safe to you. However, taking risks is a necessary part of growth. So do participate in the discussion as much as you are able.

2. Be sensitive to the other members of the group. Listen attentively when they talk. You will learn from their insights. If you can, link what you say to the comments of others so the group stays on the topic.

3. Be careful not to dominate the discussion. We are sometimes so eager to share what we have learned that we do not leave opportunity for others to respond. By all means participate! But allow others to do so as well.

4. Expect God to teach you through the passage being discussed and through the other members of the group. Pray that you will have a profitable time together.

5. We recommend that groups follow a few basic guidelines and that these guidelines be read at the beginning of each discussion session. The guidelines, which you may wish to adapt to your situation, are

☐ Anything said in the group is considered confidential and will not be discussed outside the group unless specific permission is given to do so.

☐ We will provide time for each person present to talk if he or she feels comfortable doing so.

☐ We will talk about ourselves and our own situations, avoiding conversation about other people.

☐ We will listen attentively to each other.

☐ We will be very cautious about giving advice.

☐ We will pray for each other.

If you are the discussion leader, you will find additional suggestions and helpful ideas for each study in the leader's notes. These are found at the back of the guide.

You might also want to consider participating in the online discussion forum for group leaders at <www.lettinggodbegod.com>.

1

God's Promise
of Peace

JOHN 13:34;
14:23-27

All of us want to live without anxiety. But we often look for peace in the wrong places. Maybe we will be at peace, we tell ourselves, when this next big project is done. Maybe we will be at peace when the latest stressful event is behind us. Maybe we will feel peace when other people change. Maybe when we get away, when we finally get some rest, we will find peace. But big projects and stressful events never end. Even if other people change, it doesn't always lead to reduced anxiety for us; maybe they will change back! And when we find time for rest, we may find that our "rest" is full of tension and anxiety.

It is worth emphasizing that what we want is *inner* peace. We want to be able to sustain serenity—even when external circumstances remain difficult or stressful. To do that we obviously need to explore what is going on inside. What is the root of our anxiety?

Our anxieties often grow in the soil of fears—especially the fear that we are separated in some way from God. As we will see in the text for this study, God offers us a remarkable solution to this fear. God will make his home with us.

PREPARE
Think of a time when you experienced a sense of inner peace. How would you describe what you experienced?

What are you hoping to get as a result of working through these studies on receiving peace?

READ

³⁴ *"A new command I give you: Love one another. As I have loved you, so you must love one another. (John 13:34)*

²³ *"If anyone loves me, he will obey my teaching. My Father will love him, and we will come to him and make our home with him. ²⁴He who does not love me will not obey my teaching. These words you hear are not my own; they belong to the Father who sent me.*

²⁵ *"All this I have spoken while still with you. ²⁶But the Counselor, the Holy Spirit, whom the Father will send in my name, will teach you all things and will remind you of everything I have said to you. ²⁷Peace I leave with you; my peace I give you. I do not give to you as the world gives. Do not let your hearts be troubled and do not be afraid." (John 14:23-27)*

STUDY

1. What major themes do you see in Jesus' teaching here?

2. Reread Jesus' words in John 14:26-27, inserting your name in the text as often as possible—as though Jesus were saying this directly to you. What thoughts and feelings do you have in response to hearing these words in this personal way?

3. What is the relationship between obedience and love in these verses?

4. What is the relationship between peace and love in these verses?

5. This text speaks of God the Father, the Son and the Spirit living with us. What thoughts and feelings do you have about this promise?

6. What is your experience of the relationship between living in love and living in peace?

7. Jesus encourages us to not be troubled and afraid. What things are troubling you and causing you fear?

8. How might knowing God is with you—that you are living in God's loving presence—help alleviate your fear and bring you peace?

9. How might making choices to love others more fully—and seeing this as our primary purpose in life—alleviate fear and bring peace?

10. In a moment of quiet, invite God to be at home in you this day. Be open to whatever you sense from God as you invite God's loving presence into your heart and mind. Write about your experience of praying in this way.

REFLECT

Jesus' teaching in this text reminds us that God's Spirit is with us as counselor and teacher. Ask God's Spirit this week to be your counselor and teacher. Invite God's Spirit to show you more about loving like Jesus loved and receiving God's peace.

RESPOND

Use the meditative prayer in question 10 each day this week. Keep a journal of your experience of praying in this way.

2

Removing Barriers to Peace

LUKE 12:22-34

We worry about many things. We worry that we won't have enough money. We worry about whether we are making the right decisions. We worry about other people's choices. We worry about our health. We worry about our survival. All of this worry robs us of peace.

All of us would prefer not to worry. But we don't know how to escape it. In this text Jesus suggests an alternative path. It is the path of faith and trust. Jesus reminds us of the bigger picture. The purpose of our lives is not merely to survive but to live as members of God's kingdom of love. In the text for this study Jesus invites us to let go of our worries, trust God's loving care for us and seek our true purpose in life.

PREPARE

List the things that create anxiety for you—the things you worry about. Be as specific as you can.

Which of these things, if any, are things that you have complete control over?

READ

²²*Then Jesus said to his disciples: "Therefore I tell you, do not worry about your life, what you will eat; or about your body, what you will wear. ²³Life is more than food, and the body more than clothes. ²⁴Consider the ravens: They do not sow or reap, they have no storeroom or barn; yet God feeds them. And how much more valuable you are than birds! ²⁵Who of you by worrying can add a single hour to his life? ²⁶Since you cannot do this very little thing, why do you worry about the rest?*

²⁷*"Consider how the lilies grow. They do not labor or spin. Yet I tell you, not even Solomon in all his splendor was dressed like one of these. ²⁸If that is how God clothes the grass of the field, which is here today, and tomorrow is thrown into the fire, how much more will he clothe you, O you of little faith! ²⁹And do not set your heart on what you will eat or drink; do not worry about it. ³⁰For the pagan world runs after all such things, and your Father knows that you need them. ³¹But seek his kingdom, and these things will be given to you as well.*

³²*"Do not be afraid, little flock, for your Father has been pleased to give you the kingdom. ³³Sell your possessions and give to the poor. Provide purses for yourselves that will not wear out, a treasure in heaven that will not be exhausted, where no thief comes near and no moth destroys. ³⁴For where your treasure is, there your heart will be also." (Luke 12:22-34)*

STUDY

1. What title would you give this text?

2. What reasons does Jesus give for not worrying about such important matters as our life, food, drink and clothes?

3. Which of the perspectives that Jesus gives about our anxieties do you most need to be reminded of today? Explain.

4. What specific examples can you think of that illustrate how worries rob us of peace?

5. What makes it difficult for you to trust that God will provide for you?

6. What evidence do you have that God provides for you? List whatever comes to mind.

7. In the last part of this text Jesus shifts the focus to what life is all about. How would you paraphrase what Jesus is saying about God's kingdom?

8. In practical terms, what might it mean in your life to seek God's kingdom?

9. What relationship do you see between seeking God's kingdom and finding peace?

10. Reread the text, inserting your name as often as possible. Then write about what it is like to hear Jesus' words so personally.

REFLECT
Look at your responses to questions 5 and 6. In a time of prayer, allow yourself to bring your fears to God. Offer your fears to God. Then spend some time acknowledging all the evidence you can think of that God cares for you and provides for you. Thank God for each gift of care.

RESPOND
Ask God each day this week to show you what it means for you to seek God's kingdom of love first as you go about your day. Keep a journal of the insights you gain as you watch and listen for God's response to this prayer.

3

Seeking God's Peace

PHILIPPIANS 4:6-9

We want to let go of our anxiety. We want to be open to receive God's peace. But every day we are faced with new challenges and concerns. Every day we have new reasons to be anxious and afraid. We need to know what to do when we get anxious. We need to know in practical, everyday terms how to move from fear and anxiety toward peace.

In the text for this study we will explore practical wisdom from Scripture about seeking God's peace. We will see that the first step is to know that we are anxious. We need to be aware of our fears and be willing to acknowledge them to ourselves and to God. In this way our worries become an opportunity to turn again to God. As we seek God's help, God promises us that the peace of God will guard our hearts and our minds.

PREPARE

What, in your experience, causes your fears and anxiety to increase?

What, in your experience, helps to create an inner peace?

READ

6Do not be anxious about anything, but in everything, by prayer and petition, with thanksgiving, present your requests to God. 7And the peace of God, which transcends all understanding, will guard your hearts and your minds in Christ Jesus.

8Finally, brothers, whatever is true, whatever is noble, whatever is right, whatever is pure, whatever is lovely, whatever is admirable—if anything is excellent or praiseworthy—think about such things. 9Whatever you have learned or received or heard from me, or seen in me—put it into practice. And the God of peace will be with you. (Philippians 4:6-9)

STUDY

1. Reread the text, paraphrasing it so that it reads like comforting, inviting words spoken by a loving parent to a frightened child. You may want to write out your paraphrase, keeping it simple and brief.

2. Now, put your name in the paraphrase you just wrote, so that God is speaking directly to you as a much-loved child. What thoughts and feelings do you have as you hear these words?

3. Look at the verses again. What specific steps are suggested for us when we are anxious?

4. How would doing these things help lead to peace?

5. What are you anxious or concerned about today? Express your concern to God as a written prayer, acknowledging your fears and your gratitude.

6. This text invites us to think about things that are true, noble, right, pure, lovely, admirable, excellent or praiseworthy. What comes to mind as you focus on these words?

7. As you think about your concerns, ask God to show you how you might think about the situation that concerns you in the light of what is true, noble, right, pure, lovely, admirable, excellent or praiseworthy. What comes to mind?

8. The text suggests that God's peace "transcends all understanding." That is, when we receive God's peace, we will find ourselves surprisingly peaceful even in the face of difficult circumstances. Describe a time when you have experienced this.

9. In another time of quiet allow yourself to be in the presence of the God of peace. Write about your experience in this time of prayer.

---

10. In another time of quiet, talk to God about the things which concern you the most at this time. As you do so, express your gratitude to God. Release to God whatever fears you are prepared to release. Receive from God whatever peace you are prepared to receive. Try not to spend this time evaluating how well you are doing this—release what you can release, receive what you can receive. Write about your experience during this time of prayer.

REFLECT
In a time of quiet, picture the God of peace with you as light shining on you. Picture God's light shining on you and in you, guarding your heart and mind with the gift of peace. What thoughts and feelings do you have about this image?

RESPOND
Each day this week use the prayers found in questions 9 and 10 as you reflect on your concerns about the day. Keep a journal of what you experience in these times of prayer each day.

4

Letting God Give You Peace

MATTHEW 11:28-30

We know what it is like to be in the company of friends and family who are rushed, pressured and distracted. We know what it is like to be with people who are full of themselves. We know what it is like to spend time with people who are unkind or disrespectful toward us.

Jesus invites us to a completely different kind of experience. "Come and be with me," Jesus invites us. "Come, sit down, slow down and rest with me. You will find that I am gentle. You will find that I am humble. You will find that being with me is easy. Come, find rest for your souls. For my yoke is easy and my burden is light."

PREPARE

Think of one or two people in your life (now or in the past) who were a source of peace for you. What did they do to bring peace to you?

What did you do that helped you to receive their gifts of peace?

READ

²⁸"Come to me, all you who are weary and burdened, and I will give you rest. ²⁹Take my yoke upon you and learn from me, for I am gentle and humble in heart, and you will find rest for your souls. ³⁰For my yoke is easy and my burden is light." (Matthew 11:28-30)

STUDY

1. Restate the invitation made by Jesus in this text, using your own words and putting your name in the invitation where appropriate.

2. It is important to notice that this text is an invitation, not a demand. We do have a choice about when, if and how we will respond. What is the significance to you that Jesus comes to us with an *invitation* to receive peace?

3. Jesus is inviting the weary and burdened. In what way does this sound like a description of you?

4. What is the significance of what Jesus says about himself?

How might this affect our ability to receive peace from him?

5. What experience have you had of coming to Jesus and finding rest for your soul? Describe how you went to Jesus and how you received rest.

6. In a time of quiet, pray that God will guide you as you listen again to this text. Read the text aloud again slowly, several times, putting your name in the text so you can hear Jesus inviting you to come and receive and learn.

7. What responses did you experience as you let Jesus' words speak to you?

8. In another time of quiet, respond to Jesus' invitation to be with him. Be aware of his gentleness. Let yourself rest in his love. Write about your experience in this time of prayer.

---

9. Write a prayer responding to Jesus' invitation to you.

REFLECT

In a time of quiet, again picture yourself responding to Jesus' invitation. You may see yourself literally resting with Jesus in a meadow, by a lake or in some other place. Let your body and mind relax in his presence. Stay with this image for a while. Ask him to give you soul rest. Write about your experience.

RESPOND

Use questions 6 through 9 each day this week, reflecting daily on this text. Keep a journal of your reflections.

5

Resting in God's Peace

PSALM 62

Sometimes we are able to move past our fears and our lack of trust. Sometimes we are able to receive peace from God. But often we find that the peace we experience is temporary. In a short period of time we find ourselves anxious again. Sometimes the same anxieties return—and we may even have additional anxieties about the fact that we are anxious again. It is not easy for us to maintain the serenity that God has offered to us. Fortunately, God is not surprised that the quest for peace and serenity is a long one. It comes as no shock to God that we need to return again and again to receive God's peace.

The psalm for this study invites us to come back to God—to come back to rest in God's gift of peace. The psalmist reminds us, "Trust in him at all times, O people; pour out your hearts to him, for God is our refuge."

PREPARE

If your inner peace depended on the people in your life and the choices they make or the mood they are in, what impact might this have on your inner peace?

If your inner peace depended instead on a trustworthy, strong and loving God, what impact might this have on your inner peace?

 READ

¹My soul finds rest in God alone;
    my salvation comes from him.
²He alone is my rock and my salvation;
he is my fortress, I will never be shaken.

³How long will you assault a man?
    Would all of you throw him down—
    this leaning wall, this tottering fence?
⁴They fully intend to topple him
    from his lofty place;
    they take delight in lies.
With their mouths they bless,
    but in their hearts they curse.   Selah

⁵Find rest, O my soul, in God alone;
    my hope comes from him.
⁶He alone is my rock and my salvation;
    he is my fortress, I will not be shaken.
⁷My salvation and my honor depend on God;
    he is my mighty rock, my refuge.
⁸Trust in him at all times, O people;
    pour out your hearts to him,
    for God is our refuge.   Selah

⁹Lowborn men are but a breath,
    the highborn are but a lie;
if weighed on a balance, they are nothing;
    together they are only a breath.
¹⁰Do not trust in extortion
    or take pride in stolen goods;
though your riches increase,
    do not set your heart on them.

¹¹One thing God has spoken,
  two things have I heard:
that you, O God, are strong,
¹² and that you, O Lord, are loving.
Surely you will reward each person
  according to what he has done. (Psalm 62)

STUDY

1. List all the things that the psalmist says about God in these verses.

2. What does the psalmist say about himself in relation to God?

3. What contrasts does the psalmist make between his experience with people and his experience with God?

4. The psalmist invites us to "find rest . . . in God alone," "trust in him at all times" and "pour out [our] hearts out to him." How is each of these things related to resting in God's peace?

5. Which of these things is the most difficult for you to do?

6. Which of these things have you found yourself doing more of, especially as you have been working through these studies?

7. What has the impact been in your life?

8. In a time of quiet, focus on one of the things the psalmist says about God. Ask God to show you this aspect of his character. Be open to whatever you might sense from God. When you are ready, write whatever you sensed in this time of meditative prayer.

9. Write a prayer, pouring your heart out to God about all the concerns on your heart and mind.

10. Write a prayer, thanking God for being your source of hope and rest, and for the gifts of peace God has given you.

REFLECT

Use the image of God as your rock during a time of reflective prayer. It might help to keep in mind that a large rock in the desert where the psalmist lived provided protection from sun, wind, storms, predators and enemies. What do you see in this image? Write about your thoughts and feelings.

RESPOND

Use questions 8, 9 and 10 as a focus for your prayer journal this week or for your verbal prayers. Notice the impact that praying in this way has on your ability to rest in God's peace.

6

Walking in God's Peace

ISAIAH 58:1-12

The text for this study focuses on the difference it makes to live in peace with God, self and others. As we have seen in previous studies, our fears about not having enough often rob us of the deep inner peace we desire. These same fears can lead us to make choices based in greed or choices which result in injustice. The consequence is that no peace is possible—in our relationship with ourselves, in our relationship with God and in our relationships with others.

As we will see again in this text, walking in the peace we have received from God means walking in compassion and justice. The peace of God always works toward establishing peace in our hearts, our relationships, our communities and our world.

 PREPARE

Think about the conflicts in the world at this time. What are the underlying reasons for these conflicts and wars?

Think about the conflicts in your relationships or in your heart at this time. What are the underlying reasons for these conflicts?

READ

¹ "Shout it aloud, do not hold back.
Raise your voice like a trumpet.
Declare to my people their rebellion
and to the house of Jacob their sins.
²For day after day they seek me out;
they seem eager to know my ways,
as if they were a nation that does what is right
and has not forsaken the commands of its God.
They ask me for just decisions
and seem eager for God to come near them.
³ 'Why have we fasted,' they say,
and you have not seen it?
Why have we humbled ourselves,
and you have not noticed?'

"Yet on the day of your fasting, you do as you please
and exploit all your workers.
⁴Your fasting ends in quarreling and strife,
and in striking each other with wicked fists.
You cannot fast as you do today
and expect your voice to be heard on high.
⁵Is this the kind of fast I have chosen,
only a day for a man to humble himself?
Is it only for bowing one's head like a reed
and for lying on sackcloth and ashes?
Is that what you call a fast,
a day acceptable to the LORD?

⁶ "Is not this the kind of fasting I have chosen:
to loose the chains of injustice
and untie the cords of the yoke,
to set the oppressed free
and break every yoke?

> [7]*Is it not to share your food with the hungry*
>   *and to provide the poor wanderer with shelter—*
> *when you see the naked, to clothe him,*
>   *and not to turn away from your own flesh and blood?*
> [8]*Then your light will break forth like the dawn,*
>   *and your healing will quickly appear;*
> *then your righteousness will go before you,*
>   *and the glory of the* LORD *will be your rear guard.*
> [9]*Then you will call, and the* LORD *will answer;*
> *you will cry for help, and he will say: Here am I.*

> *"If you do away with the yoke of oppression,*
>   *with the pointing finger and malicious talk,*
> [10]*and if you spend yourselves in behalf of the hungry*
>   *and satisfy the needs of the oppressed,*
> *then your light will rise in the darkness,*
>   *and your night will become like the noonday.*
> [11]*The* LORD *will guide you always;*
>   *he will satisfy your needs in a sun-scorched land*
>   *and will strengthen your frame.*
> *You will be like a well-watered garden,*
>   *like a spring whose waters never fail.*
> [12]*Your people will rebuild the ancient ruins*
>   *and will raise up the age-old foundations;*
> *you will be called Repairer of Broken Walls,*
>   *Restorer of Streets with Dwellings." (Isaiah 58:1-12)*

STUDY

1. How would you summarize the way of life that is being described in the first five verses of this text?

2. How would you summarize the way of life being described in verses 6 through 12?

3. Review the passage from John's Gospel in the first study in this guide. What parallels do you see between Jesus' teaching in the text from John's Gospel and the message of this text?

4. What specifically does this text call us to do?

5. What does this text say will be the result in our own lives of taking these actions?

6. What is the practical significance of these promised results?

7. In a time of quiet ask God to show you anything God wants you to correct or change in your life, particularly in your relationships with other people. Write about your experience in this time of prayer.

8. Write a prayer asking God to strengthen you to walk in his love, justice and peace with others.

9. In another time of quiet, reflect on the promise "you will be called Repairer of Broken Walls, Restorer of Streets with Dwellings." Ask God to show you how you might be used as a repairer and restorer. Write about your experience in this time of prayer.

---

10. Spend some time reflecting on how you have put the truths of these studies into action. What growth do you see in your capacity to receive peace from God?

REFLECT

Spend some time reflecting on the metaphors of light in verses 8 and 10. Write about your thoughts in response to these images.

RESPOND

Use the prayers in questions 7 and 9 each day this week. Write whatever you sense God is showing you each day. Make a plan to respond to what God is showing you about your life.

LEADER'S NOTES

You may be experiencing a variety of feelings as you anticipate leading a group through this study guide. You may feel inadequate for the task and afraid of what will happen. If this is the case, know you are in good company. Many other small group leaders share this experience. It may help you to know that your willingness to lead is a gift to the other group members. It might also help if you tell them about your feelings and ask them to pray for you. Realize as well that the other group members share the responsibility for the group. And realize that it is the Spirit's work to bring insight, comfort, healing and recovery to group members. Your role is simply to provide guidance to the discussion. The suggestions listed below will help you to provide that guidance.

Preparing to Lead

1. Develop realistic expectations of yourself as a small group leader. Do not feel that you have to "have it all together." Rather, commit yourself to an ongoing discipline of honesty about your own needs. As you grow in honesty about your own needs, you will grow as well in your capacity for compassion, gentleness and patience with yourself and with others. As a leader you can encourage an atmosphere of honesty by being honest about yourself.

2. Pray. Pray for yourself. Pray for the group members. Invite the Spirit to be present as you prepare and as you meet.

3. Read the text several times.

4. Take your time to thoughtfully work through each question, writing out your answers.

5. After completing your personal study, read through the leader's notes for the study you are leading. These notes are designed to help you in several ways. First, they tell you the purpose the authors had in mind while writing the study. Take time to think through how the questions work together to accomplish that purpose. Second, the notes provide you with additional background information or comments on some of the questions. This information can be useful when people have difficulty understanding or answering a question. Third, the leader's notes can alert you to potential problems you may encounter during the study.

6. If you wish to remind yourself during the group discussion of anything mentioned in the leader's notes, make a note to yourself below that question in your study guide.

Leading the Study

1. Begin on time. You may want to open in prayer, or have a group member do so.

2. Be sure everyone has a study guide. Decide as a group whether you want people to do the study on their own ahead of time. If your time together is limited, it will be helpful for people to prepare in advance.

3. At the beginning of your first time together, explain that these studies are meant to be discussions, not lectures. Encourage the members of the group to participate. However, do not put pressure on those who may be hesitant to speak during the first few sessions. Clearly state that people do not need to share anything they do not feel safe sharing. Remind people that it will take time to trust each other.

4. Read aloud the group guidelines listed in the front of the guide. These commitments are important in creating a safe place for people to talk and trust and feel.

5. Read aloud the introductory paragraphs at the beginning of the discussion for the day. This will orient the group to the passage being studied.

6. If the group does not prepare in advance, approximately ten minutes will be needed for individuals to work on the "Prepare" section. This is designed to help group members focus on some aspect of their personal experience. Hopefully it will help group members to be more aware of the frame of reference and life experience that we bring to the text. This time of personal reflection can be done prior to the group meeting or as the first part of the meeting. The prepare questions are not designed to be for group discussion, but you might begin by asking the group what they learned from the prepare questions.

7. Read the passage aloud. You may choose to do this yourself, or someone else may read if he or she has been asked to do so prior to the study.

8. As you begin to ask the questions in the guide, keep several things in mind. First, the questions are designed to be used just as they are written. If you wish, you may simply read them aloud to the group. Or you may prefer to express them in your own words. However, unnecessary rewording of the questions is not recommended.

Second, the questions are intended to guide the group toward understanding and applying the main idea of the study. The authors of the guide have stated the purpose of each study in the leader's notes. You should try to understand how the study questions and the biblical text work together to lead the group in that direction.

There may be times when it is appropriate to deviate from the study guide. For example, a question may have already been answered. If so, move on to the next question. Or someone may raise an important question not covered in the guide. Take time to discuss it! The important thing is to use discretion. There may be many routes you can travel to reach the goal of the study. But the easiest route is usually the one the authors have suggested.

9. Don't be afraid of silence. People need time to think about the question before formulating their answers.

10. Don't be content with just one response. Ask, "What do the rest of you think?" or "Anything else?" until several people have given answers to the question.

11. Acknowledge all contributions. Try to be affirming whenever possible. Never reject an answer. If it seems clearly wrong to you, ask: "Which part of the text led you to that conclusion?" or "What do the rest of you think?"

12. Don't expect every answer to be addressed to you, even though this will probably happen at first. As group members become more at ease, they will begin to interact more effectively with each other. This is a sign of a healthy discussion.

13. Don't be afraid of controversy. It can be very stimulating. Differences can enrich our lives. If you don't resolve an issue completely, don't be frustrated. Move on and keep it in mind for later. A subsequent study may resolve the problem.

14. Stick to the passage under consideration. It should be the source for answering the questions. Discourage the group from unnecessary cross-referencing. Likewise, stick to the subject and avoid going off on tangents.

15. Periodically summarize what the group has said about the topic. This helps to draw together the various ideas mentioned and gives continuity to the study. But be careful not to use summary statements as an opportunity to give a sermon!

16. End each study with a prayer time. You will want to draw on the themes of your study and individual prayer and meditation as you now pray together. There are several ways to handle this time in a group. The person who leads each study could lead the group in a prayer, or you could allow time for group participation. Remember that some members of your group may feel uncomfortable about participating in public prayer. It might be helpful to discuss this with the group during your first meeting and to reach some agreement about how to proceed.

Listening to Emotional Pain

These Bible study guides are designed to take seriously the pain and struggle that is part of life. People will experience a variety of emotions during these studies. Part of your role as group leader will be to listen to emotional pain. Listening is a gift that you can give to a person who is hurting. For many people it is not an easy gift to give. The following suggestions will help you to listen more effectively to people in emotional pain.

1. Remember that you are not responsible to take the pain away. People in helping relationships often feel that they are being asked to make the other person feel better. This is usually related to the helper's own anxiety about painful feelings.

2. Not only are you not responsible to take the pain away, but one of the things people need most is an opportunity to face and to experience the pain in their life. They may have spent years denying their pain and running from it. Healing can come when we are able to face our pain in the presence of someone who cares about us. Rather than trying to take the pain away, then, commit yourself to listening attentively as it is expressed.

3. Realize that some group members may not feel comfortable with others' expressions of sadness or anger. You may want to acknowledge that such emotions are uncomfortable but that part of the growth process is to learn to feel and allow others to feel.

4. Be very cautious about giving answers and advice. Advice and answers may make you feel better or competent, but they may also minimize peoples' problems and their painful feelings. Simple solutions rarely work, and they can easily communicate "You should be better now" or "You shouldn't really be talking about this."

5. Be sure to communicate direct affirmation any time people talk about their painful emotions. It takes courage to talk about our pain because it creates anxiety for us. It is a great gift to be trusted by those who are struggling.

Study Notes

The following notes refer to the questions in the Bible study portion of each study.

Study 1. God's Promise of Peace. John 13:34; 14:23-27.

Purpose: To hear Jesus' invitation to receive God's peace.

Question 1. The themes in this text are love, obedience, a promise of God the

Father, Son and Spirit living with us, and a promise of peace.

Question 2. You might want to encourage participants to read these verses aloud in this way in pairs, or go around the group reading in this way, depending on the size of your group.

Question 3. Before Jesus' death he had a long, intimate conversation with his followers. The focus of this conversation was to address their needs and concerns in anticipation of his death. He went over the basics with them. "I've taught you one thing; remember that one thing, do that one thing—love each other. To live in love is to live in God."

It is possible that some group members may read the words "obey my teaching" and become anxious about keeping all the rules and doing everything right. It is also possible that when it becomes clear that the teaching Jesus is talking about is his central teaching to love each other, some might become anxious about loving enough, or may confuse the teaching to love others with fears about trying harder. Remind participants that Scripture teaches us that we grow in love. Each day, each hour, as we choose to love, we invite God's life to be greater in us, and each hour, as we invite God to live in us, our capacity to act in love toward others increases.

Question 4. The relationship between peace and love is that peace grows in the soil of love. Jesus is talking to people for whom *religion* and *God* and *law* have all become pretty much synonymous and for whom obeying God is the ultimate value. Jesus says to them that God's law consists of one commandment: it is the commandment to love. These were radical words in the ears of his audience. "If you want to obey God, then obey this one thing," Jesus says. "Love each other." "When you choose love, you are choosing God, you are inviting God—my Father, myself, and the Spirit—to live in you. We will make our home with you," Jesus says. "And this tender, powerful, loving union will be the source of peace in your life."

Question 5. This is an incredible, outrageous promise! Our Maker, our God, promises to live with us. What greater source of security could there be than this? The One who is love, who sustains all things, lives with us.

Note that Jesus says that as we obey the command to love, God loves us and will live with us. Jesus does not say that God does not love us when we fail at love or choose not to love. This is the language of lovers. God is the Lover who initiates. God wants us. God waits for us. God calls to us in love. Jesus is saying that when we respond to God's call of love, we are inviting God to the deeply intimate relationship God wants to have with us, and that God will come to us and unite with us in love and will live with us.

Question 6. Encourage participants to think of practical expressions of these truths. These truths can too easily be made into abstractions, but they are not abstract truths. They are real, life-changing, practical truths. These truths show up in big and little ways in our lives. Encourage whatever examples people think of from their own experience.

Question 8. When a child is afraid, a parent comforts the child with his or her supportive, protective presence: "I am here; I will take care of you; I will help you." The child is comforted and calmed. Our Maker, our good and compassionate Parent, whose love and power are infinite, is with us. What greater comfort and security could there be in all the universe? Encourage participants to think of ways this reality might help them as they face the things that are troubling to them in life at this time.

Question 9. When we understand that love is what life is about—that learning to love like Jesus loved is the central purpose and joy in life—it becomes the orienting value, the center, of all we do and are. This clarity about life's purpose can contribute to our internal experience of peace because many of the things that cause us anxiety are not important compared to love.

Question 10. Allow group participants a few minutes alone to pray and write. Invite any that want to, to share their experience during this time of meditative prayer.

Study 2. Removing Barriers to Peace. Luke 12:22-34.

Purpose: To explore the perspectives and fears that are barriers to peace.

Question 1. The purpose of this question is to help participants get an overview of the text. Encourage a variety of titles.

Question 2. Jesus says we do not need to worry about our life, food, drink or clothes because (1) worrying about the length of our life will not add even an hour to it; that is, we have no control over the outcome so it is a waste of our energies; (2) God provides for the birds and the flowers and will certainly provide for us; (3) life is not about acquiring these things—in spite of the fact that they are necessary things. The things we worry about are not the point of life, and we can get so caught up in them that we miss life all together.

Questions 3-4. Encourage participants to respond to Jesus' teachings as they apply to their specific struggles and anxieties.

Question 5. We all have distorted beliefs and fears that make it difficult for us to trust God. We may think God is too busy or that we are not important enough for God to pay attention to our concerns. We may think that God only provides for people who have been really good.

Question 6. It is very useful to remember how God has provided for us in the past. This can open our hearts and minds to the possibility of trusting God more fully in the present.

Question 7. God's kingdom is a place where love that is an active, providing, caring reality dwells. God provides for us out of love and invites us to provide for others out of love. Pursuing opportunities to love in practical ways is what life is about, Jesus says. This is life's meaning, life's joy, life's treasure. When our focus is on God's kingdom—on spiritual treasure, on seeking opportunities to love—we will not worry so much about what we have or don't have.

Question 8. Encourage participants to be as specific and practical as they can be as they relate this teaching to their current lives.

Question 9. To seek God's kingdom—to seek opportunities to love—is to know life's true meaning and joy. It is to live in direct, conscious relationship with God, who is the source of all peace.

Question 10. You might want to give participants a few minutes alone to do this, or have them pair up and take turns reading the text aloud to each other.

Study 3. Seeking God's Peace. Philippians 4:6-9.

Purpose: To hear God's practical wisdom about seeking peace.

Question 1. Allow people time to write their own version of this text as if it were being said to a child. Encourage them to make the language simple and understandable.

Question 2. Allow participants a chance to actually do this. You may want to break into pairs. This text is a generous, loving invitation by God to us to come with anything and everything. We are God's dearly loved children. God wants to help us with our fears and concerns. God wants to meet our needs.

Question 3. It is useful to look at each step: (1) acknowledging that we are anxious, (2) taking our concerns to God, (3) doing so with thanksgiving (gratitude and hope), (4) letting God's peace replace the fear and anxiety, and (5) focusing on the good, the presence of God, the evidence of God at work.

Question 4. We open ourselves to the gift of peace when we learn to take every concern to God. Our fears and anxieties become reminders of our need for God and of God's eagerness to help. We open ourselves to receiving God's peace when we are grateful—when we notice and take in God's provision and protection and say thank you. And we open ourselves to receiving God's peace when we focus on God's work and God's presence in this world—when we focus on the light rather than on the darkness.

Question 5. Allow each person time to write and pray silently. Some may want to read their prayers; others may want to keep them private.

Question 6. The things in this list to think about are things which are good—

things which are evidence of God's goodness and love in this world. Reflecting on God's active, loving presence with us helps us to remember what we forget when we are anxious—that God is always with us, always working in our circumstances.

Question 7. Encourage participants to apply their reflections on God's good and loving presence with them to their specific fears and concerns.

Question 8. Sharing experiences of receiving God's peace in past circumstances can be an encouragement to trust that this experience is possible in the present or the future.

Questions 9-10. Allow participants time to pray and reflect individually. Invite any that want to share their experience in this time of prayer to do so.

Study 4. Letting God Give You Peace. Matthew 11:28-30.

Purpose: To respond to Jesus' invitation to find rest with him.

Question 1. Encourage people to make their summaries simple, direct and personal. Give each person an opportunity to read his or her personalized version of this invitation.

Question 2. Participants may have a variety of responses to this question. Some may be moved by the fact that it is an invitation, rather than a demand. Some may be moved by the fact that Jesus invites them to come to him. Some may be touched by the fact that the peace they are seeking is being offered as a gift by Jesus.

Question 3. Encourage participants to share whatever they are comfortable expressing about themselves physically, emotionally, spiritually and relationally. You may want to lead the way by sharing personally from your own life.

Question 4. Jesus says, "I am gentle and humble in heart." When we come to him and get to know him, we will discover his gentleness, his humility (respect, compassion, empathy are all a part of humility). Jesus says we will find rest for our souls. He says "My yoke is easy and my burden is light." Participants are likely to have a variety of responses to these words. Encourage participants to compare and contrast these words with what they expect God to say to them when they are anxious.

Question 6. For questions 6-9 allow participants some time alone. They may need fifteen to twenty minutes. Encourage participants to begin by asking for God to quiet their hearts and minds and to help them be open to hear God's word to them. You may want to offer time when you come back together for people to talk about what they experienced.

Study 5. Resting in God's Peace. Psalm 62.

Purpose: To continue to seek and receive God's peace.

Question 1. The psalmist says that God is the source of salvation, a rock and a fortress, a refuge, strong and loving.

Question 2. The psalmist says that he finds rest in God and only in God; he will never be shaken because of God; his hope comes from God; he calls others (and himself) to trust in God at all times and to pour our hearts out to God.

Question 3. The psalmist describes people who are trying to topple him, who lie, who pretend to bless while they are really cursing him inwardly. He also describes the impermanence of people. In contrast he describes God as trustworthy, on our side, loving, strong, immovable, protective, absolutely reliable.

Question 4. Resting in God, trusting in God and pouring out our hearts to God are all aspects of receiving peace from God that we have explored in earlier studies. It can be helpful to review these basics over and over.

Question 8. Allow participants time to respond to questions 8-10 on their own. As you get back together you may want to invite them to share with the group anything they choose from this time.

Study 6. Walking in God's Peace. Isaiah 58:1-12.

Purpose: To explore what it is like to live in peace with God, with ourselves and with others.

Question 1. The first five verses describe people who are religious. They are careful about observing certain rules of worship. But they do not live in love and justice. They pursue their own gain at others' expense. They are violent. They exploit their workers.

Question 2. The second half of the text describes a way of life characterized by love and justice. It describes acts of compassion, kindness and respect for others in need.

Question 4. The text calls us to loose the chains of injustice, to untie the cords of the yoke, to set the oppressed free, to break every yoke, to share our food with the hungry, to clothe the naked, to not turn away from our own flesh and blood, to do away with oppression, to do away with the pointing of the finger, to spend ourselves on behalf of the hungry, to satisfy the needs of the oppressed. (It is important to realize the emotionally, spiritually and physically needy are among the depressed and hungry.)

Question 5. The poetry of the text is powerful. The results in our lives when we live lives of active love are many. The text tells us that our light will break forth like the dawn. Our light will rise in the darkness and our night will become noonday. Our healing will quickly appear. We will call to God and God will answer. The Lord will guide us. God will satisfy our needs and strengthen our frame. We will be like a well-watered garden, a spring whose waters never fail. We will be called Repairer of Broken Walls, Restorer of Streets with Dwellings.

Question 6. Explore these powerful word pictures together. Some group members may share stories about how they have experienced these results in their own lives.

Question 7. Give participants time to work individually on questions 8-10. Invite any that want to share from their time of prayer to do so.

Question 10. You may want to use this as a time of celebration and closure for the group.

Online Resources

If you would like to share your experience using this Bible study with other people, we invite you to join us online at

<www.lettinggodbegod.com>

At the website you will be able to sign up to receive a free daily meditation written by Dale and Juanita Ryan.

Additional resources of interest to some users of these studies can be found at the online home of the Ryans:

<www.christianrecovery.com>